SOCCONINI

*Organize your work in 5 steps*

# 5S

# PRACTICAL GUIDE TO IMPROVE QUALITY AND PRODUCTIVITY

SOCCONINI

*Organize your work in 5 steps*

# 5S

# PRACTICAL GUIDE TO IMPROVE QUALITY AND PRODUCTIVITY

## LUIS SOCCONINI
## MARCO BARRANTES

SOCCONINI

5S Practical guide to improve quality and productivity
Organize your work in 5 steps.

Collection: Gestiona
Publishing director: Adrià Gibernau
1st edition 2005, Grupo Editorial Norma
2nd edition 2023, Socconini Publishing. ISBN 979-8379-34018-6
3rd edition October, 2023, Marge Books



Publisher: Marge Books
Brutau, 160, 1.º D - 08203 Sabadell (Barcelona)
Tel. +34 931 429 486 - marge@margebooks.com
www.margebooks.com

*Editorial management:* Bernardo González.
*Edition:* GalaxiaLiteraria.com / PuntoyComaEditores.com, servicios editoriales.
*Illustrations:* Jorge Díaz Barajas.
*Cover image:* Depositphotos.
*Printed by:* Safekat, SL (Madrid)

ISBN printed edition: 978-84-19109-49-1
ISBN digital edition: 978-84-19109-50-7
Legal deposit: B 16735-2023

# The authors

LUIS SOCCONINI

He is an industrial engineer from ITESM, Guadalajara campus. He has a master's degree in Quality and Productivity and is a Master Black Belt.

He is Certified in *Strategic Management* by Stanford University, in *Leading Product Innovation* by Harvard University and in *Industry 4.0* by M.I.T.

He has worked for the Wharton, Pennsylvania, business school as a business consultant; at the Grolsch Brewery in the Netherlands as a process engineer, and at IBM as a manufacturing engineer.

As director of the Lean Six Sigma Institute, he develops high impact projects in companies such as Abbott Laboratories, Kraft Heinz, Coca Cola, BMW, Bimbo, Fender, among others. He constantly develops productivity applications in diverse industries such as construction, mining, agriculture, government, energy, services, etc.

He has been a distinguished professor at several prestigious universities in Mexico.

He is the author of the books *Lean Company*, *Lean Manufacturing*, and *The 5S Process in Action*, as well as co-author of the books *Lean Six Sigma Management System for Leading Companies* and *Lean Energy 4.0*.

## MARCO BARRANTES

He is a Chemical Engineer from the Universidad Autónoma de  Guadalajara. He has a Specialty in Didactic Competencies, a Master's Degree in Quality Systems, a Doctorate in Human Development Sciences and is a Master Black Belt.

He has more than 25 years of experience collaborating in world-class manufacturing companies: Technicolor, Jabil, Trend Technologies, Kodak, Panasonic, Sanmina and Cervecería Modelo.

Postgraduate Professor in Manufacturing and Quality: Universidad Panamericana, Universidad de Guadalajara, Universidad del Valle de Atemajac and Universidad Autónoma de Guadalajara.

He has participated as Evaluator of the National Quality Award and the Jalisco Award for Quality.

# Acknowledgments

Thanks to our families for being the basis and source of inspiration in our lives.

We want to thank our friends, clients, and students. Their valuable support encourages our continuous improvement.

Special recognition to the companies that participated in the case studies in this book. Thank you for allowing us to share your experiences contributing to developing the ideas and methods exposed in this book.

# Table of contents

# Preface

Today's business environment is increasingly complex. It's characterized by its dynamism and intense competition. This coupled with globalization generates more opportunities but also increases the number of participants on the playing field.

This scenario reminds industry leaders to work with all available means to produce the tools required for daily improvement.

Sometimes, companies modify frequently in the search for improvement, and changes are required to assimilate in the shortest time. However, these adjustments usually increase stress in new organizations and generate opposite results to the initial development goals.

5S is a method that allows you to strengthen your base. The method offers a practical and straightforward way to apply fundamental quality principles to reinforce the foundations in your organization, and enable your company's operations and rhythm to move in an environment of permanent changes without affecting their health.

This book provides you with a comprehensive package of solutions. First, it teaches you what the 5S method is. Also, it helps to develop your project, providing you with educational material to train your colleagues. It includes complete guides to create support material that your company needs and, finally, software that facilitates the project's administration.

The package of solutions offered has a history of success in various organizations. That's why we're sure that you can apply it immediately to improve your work environment. If you wish, you can use it on a personal level. Remember that the best tool is the one you use.

So, we invite you to start working on your 5S project and enjoy its benefits.

*One of the benefits we experienced when implementing 5S was that our factory was always impeccable, it looked like an exhibition, we were able to show the people who visited us where and how we make our products.*

Lorenzo González
*Operations manager*
*Technicolor Guadalajara*

# Introduction

In the world of business, we usually face problems like:

- Delays in product deliveries.
- Errors in production processes.
- Accidents.
- Dirty and disorganized work areas.

How can we avoid them?

Should we get used to living with these problems?

Japan developed a system known as the 5S that allows for organized, clean, safe and above all, productive work areas.

For Japanese companies, implementing the 5S is a mandatory first step towards a total quality philosophy.

Processes with:

* Zero accidents.
* Zero defects.
* Zero delays.
* Zero waste.

Are possible as long as you have the support of an operations structured under the 5S system.

Besides all the benefits 5S offers, it is also simple, practical, and economical.

As we previously defined it, it is a system designed to maintain an organized, clean, safe, and above all, productive working area..

5S has its origin from five Japanese words that begin with the letter "S":

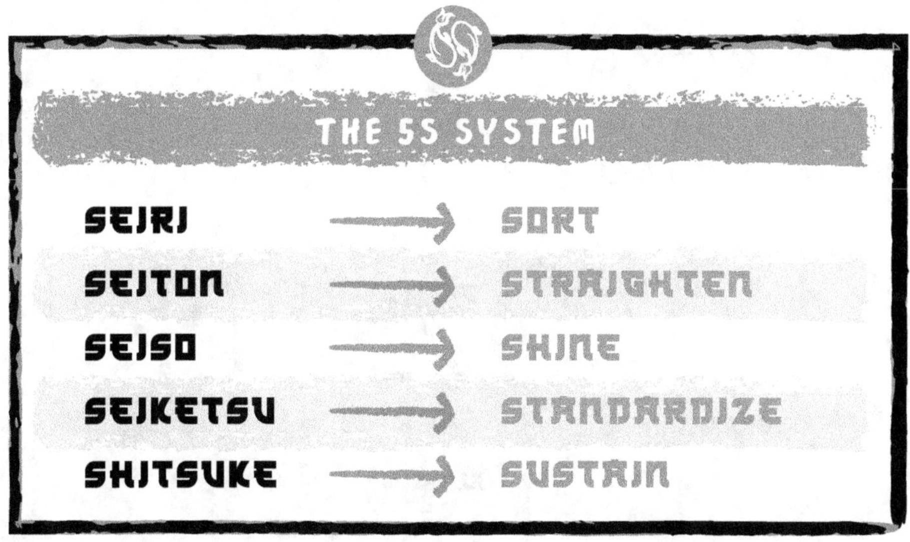

- **SEIRI** (Sort) To remove from our work area everything we don't need to carry out our production operations.

- **SEITON** (Straighten) To arrange the required articles in the correct form to facilitate their location, use, and identification, to later return them to their place of origin.

- **SEISO** (Shine) To keep our working tools in the right conditions and maintain a clean environment.

- **SEIKETSU** (Standardize) To define a consistent way to carry out the selection, organization, and cleaning.

- **SHITSUKE** (Sustain) To create conditions that encourage the organization's commitment to form habits related to the 5S activities.

# Seiri (Sort)

Look at your work area.  Pay attention to every detail.

Ask yourself:

Do you need everything that's there?

Are there objects that you don't use?

And among the essential items:

Are they the right amount?

Are they the ones you use most often?

Are they always available?

## Sort

---

*Defined as removing all non-essential articles from
a work area.*

These are the steps we must follow to remove unnecessary items from our work area.

This list can help us detect areas or objects that could go unnoticed.

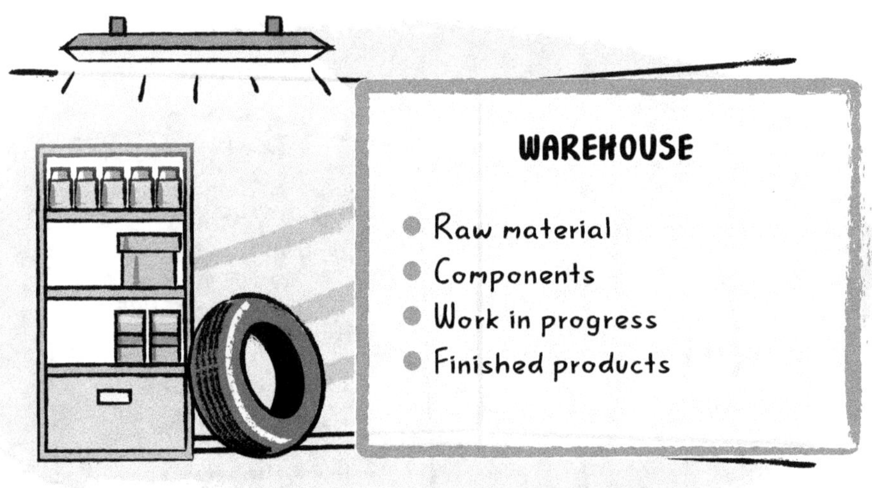


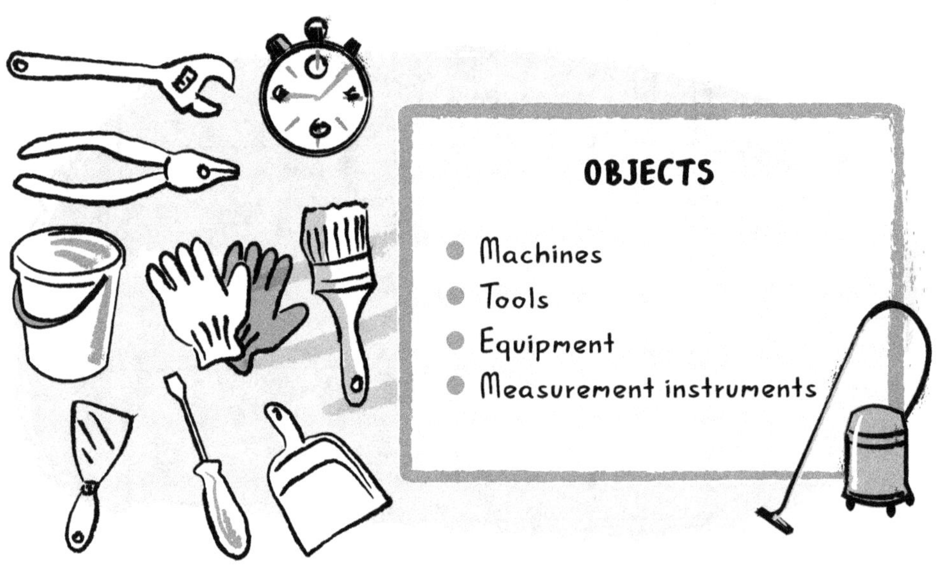

## STEP 2: DEFINE THE SELECTION CRITERIA

It's essential to establish a standard that'll help us to separate the relevant from the trivial. Here are some criteria that may be helpful to you:

- On the basis of time.

▶ Select as **necessary** everything required during a month's work.

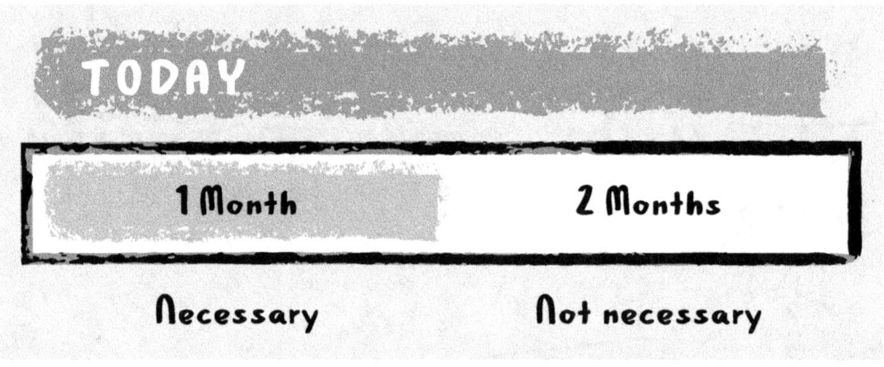


▶ Select as **unnecessary** everything not used during the past month.

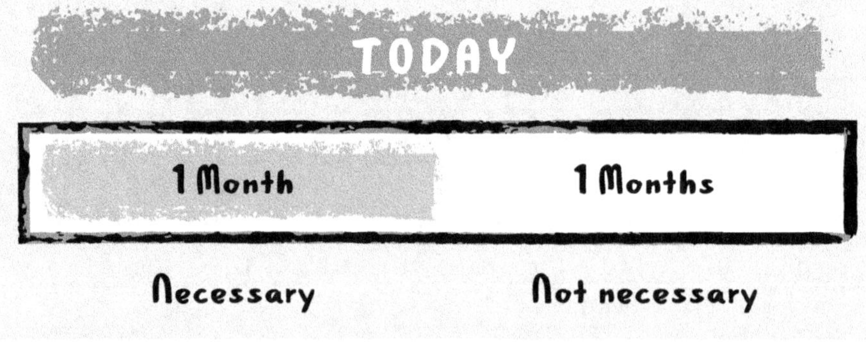

- On the basis of **frequency** of use.

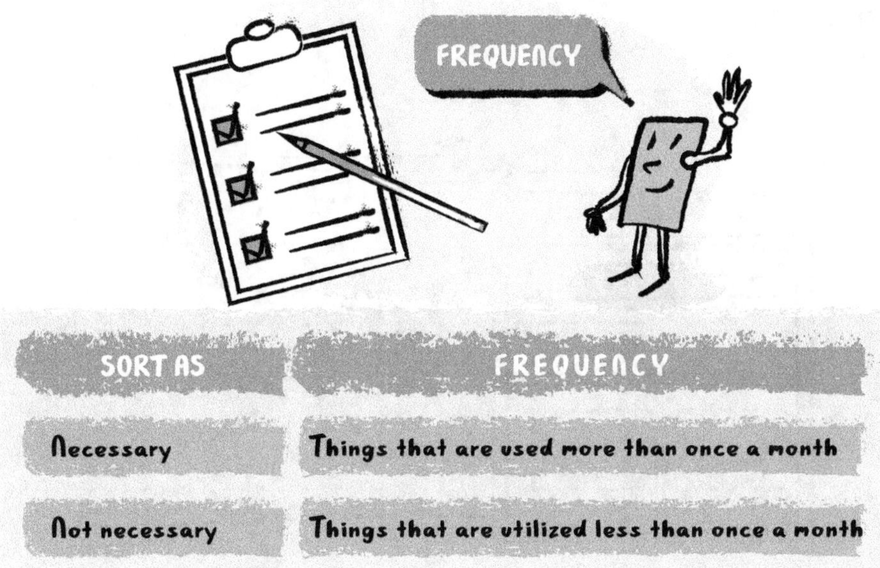


| SORT AS | FREQUENCY |
| --- | --- |
| Necessary | Things that are used more than once a month |
| Not necessary | Things that are utilized less than once a month |

- On the basis of the **amount** to use.

▶ Select as **unnecessary** the surplus created in the work area.

Identify and confine objects selected as unnecessary in a quarantined area.

## STEP 4: EVALUATE THE SELECTED OBJECTS

At this stage, we must decide what to do with the objects selected as unnecessary, asking the following questions::

- Are they excessive?
- Are they outdated?
- Are they damaged?

Use the diagram below to decide what to do with the objects selected as unnecessary.

Follow the path to the answer that corresponds to the asked questions.

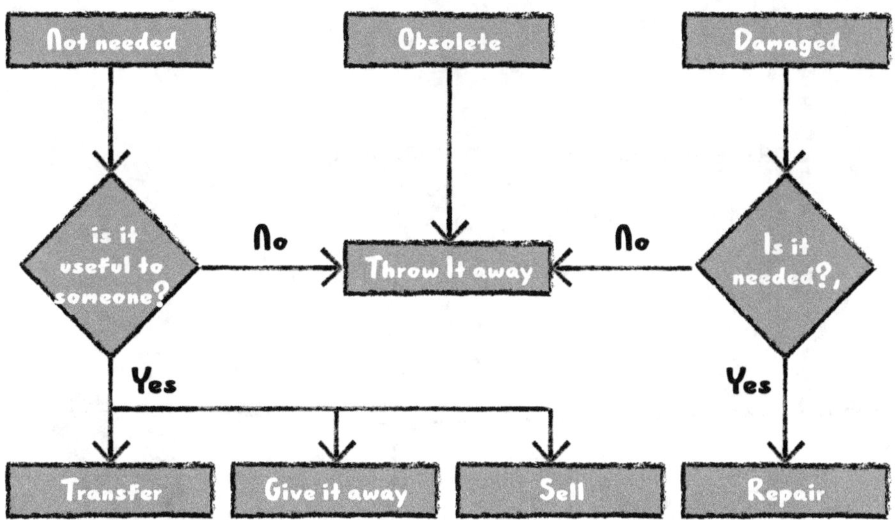

The following areas are places where unnecessary items are frequently stored:

- Unassigned places (common areas).
- Semi-hidden places.
- Closed places.

▶ *Don't forget to look in the following places.*

Upon completion of this stage you'll realize that by having only the essential items in your work area you will experience the following benefits:

* More space.
* Less clutter of unnecessary things.
* Lower inventory cost by not having extra items (only the amount required).

Remember that Seiri (select) is:

# Seiton (Straighten)

Most of us have gone through, on more than one occasion, some of the following situations:

- Wasting time searching for an item we urgently need.
- Having an accident when tripping over an object that was out of place.
- Making a mistake on the street due to a lack of signs that indicate the road.

## ORGANIZATION PROCESS

The path we must follow to organize our work area is to:

## Step 1: Prepare the work area

The first step of the organization process is to divide our work area into manageable sections that anyone can identify.

## Map (lay-out)

- ▶ Use the columns or some other reference to divide the work area into zones.
- ▶ Draw horizontal and vertical lines and identify their relationship using letters and numbers.

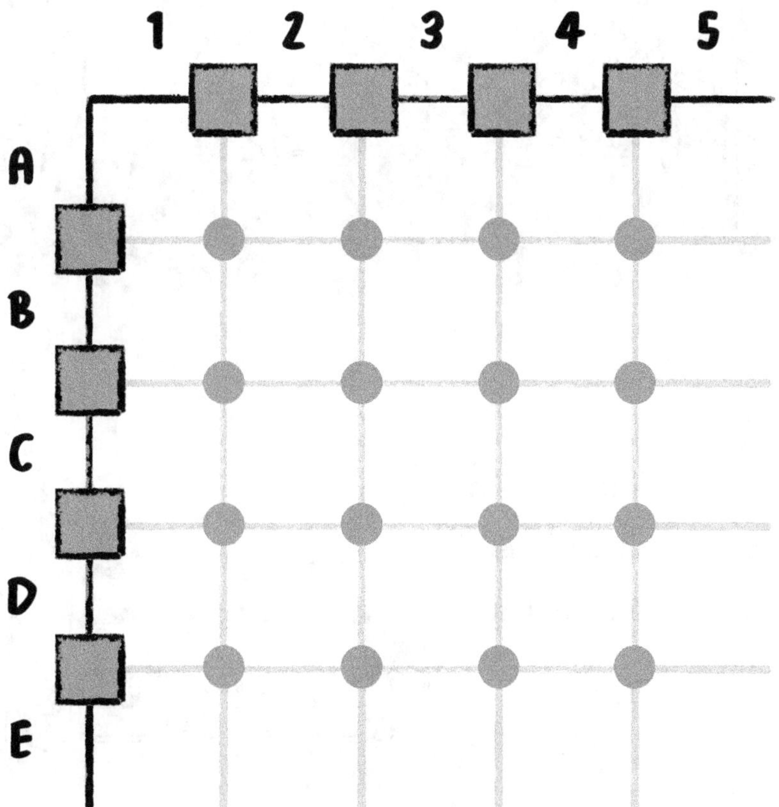

To have a good harvest, farmers usually fertilize their land before sowing. In the same manner, we recommend preparing your work area with visual aids before you start reordering any items to ensure a successful 5S project.

## Color code

The use of different paint colors is a standard visual aid. It's practical and easy to implement.

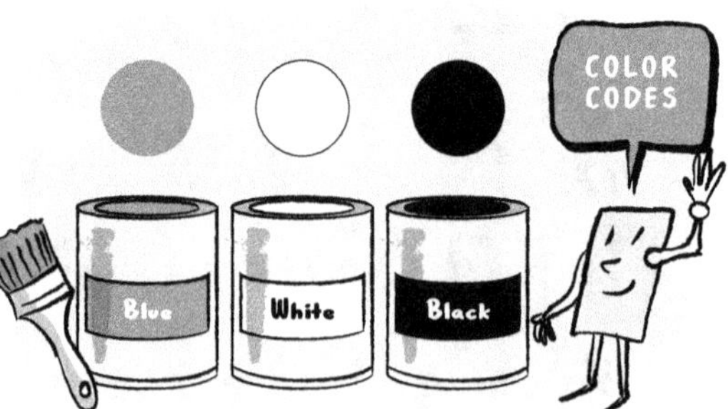

The floors use different colors according to the function that is defined for each area.

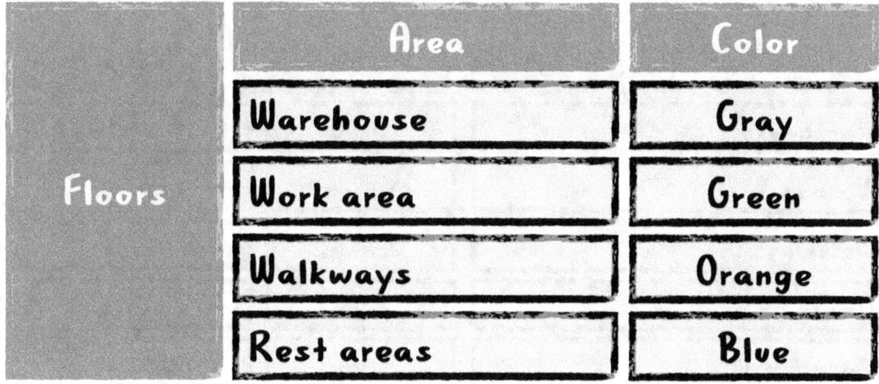



The following is an example of a stamped parts production area.

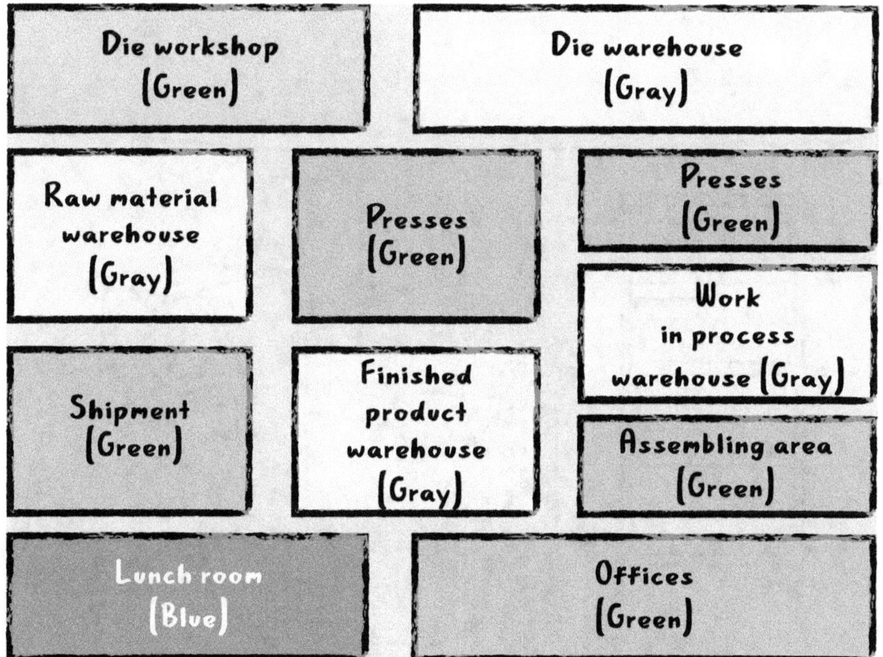

The use of tape can apply for dividing lines, and the color selection goes according to the type of division required.

| Use | Color | Characteristic |
| --- | --- | --- |
| Warehouse | Grey | Black lines |
| Work area | Green | Green |
| Walkways | Orange | Orange |
| Direction of door | Blue | Blue |
| Warehouse | Grey | Black lines |
| Work area | Green | Green |
| Walkways | Orange | Orange |
| Direction of door | Blue | Blue |

## Signs

You can use boards, blackboards, labels, or some other means to identify working areas appropriately.

Remember that signs must be in visible places, and the captions must be clear to facilitate reading.

To have an organized work area where anyone immediately can see, take, and return any item is the equivalent of responding correctly to the following three questions:

| | |
|---|---|
| **What do I need?** | Define which items are necessary (select) |
| | Identify the items |
| **Where can I find them?** | Define their correct location |
| | Mark their location to make them identifiable |
| **How many items are there?** | Define the quantity of items |
| | Identify the number of items needed |

## What do I need?

In the Selection stage (Seiri), we define which items are necessary in our work area.

Regarding identifying the necessary items, use pairs of removable labels containing the same information and place them onto the item and the container where it's stored.

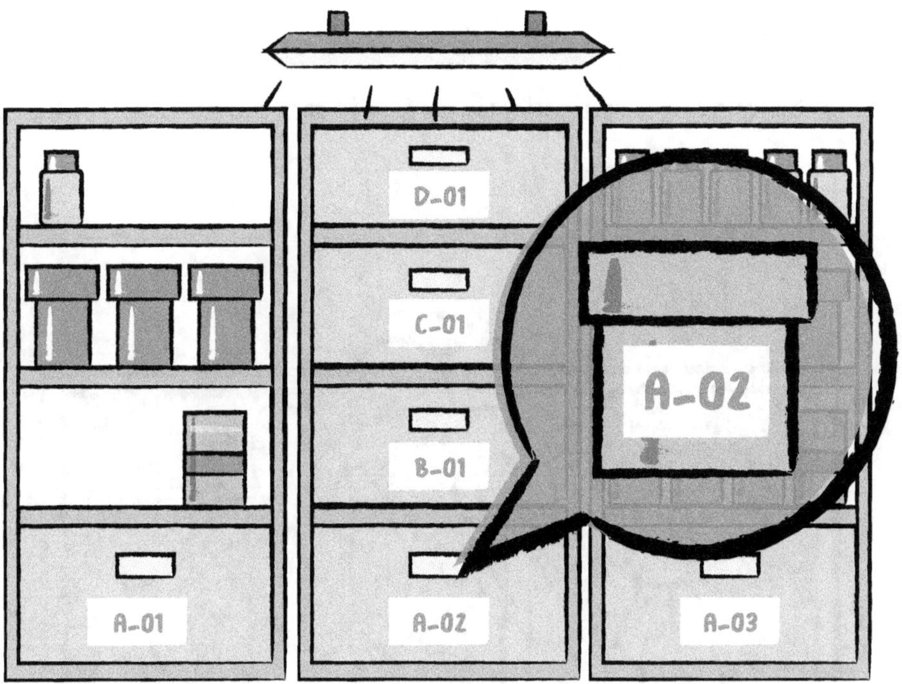


The main information on the labels is the name and the item's part number.

The following principles can help you decide the appropriate location for each item:

- Place items in the work area according to the frequency of use.

▶ Frequent use. Near the workplace.

▶ Occasional use. Not required Items near the active area.

- Store items used collectively in the same area. If possible, in the order of need.

- Store items that have a similar function in the same area.

- Avoid storing items under lock.

Proper identification of the place where the items are stored makes it easy for anyone to locate what they need and ultimately return the said item(s) after using them.

▶ Identify the cabinets.

* Use Roman numerals to identify existing cabinets in the work area.
* Divide the cabinets into columns and rows.
* Use letters to identify columns and numbers for the rows.

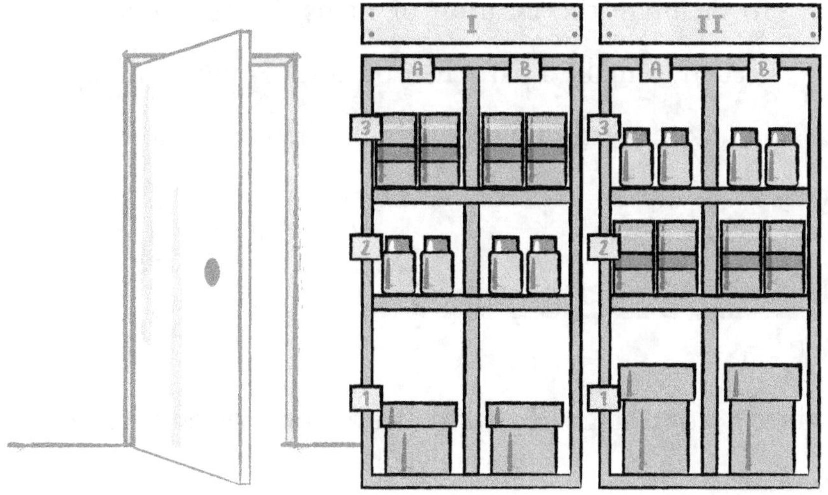

▶ Draw the outline.

• Outlining a tool is a practical and straightforward way to show its location.

▶ Color code.

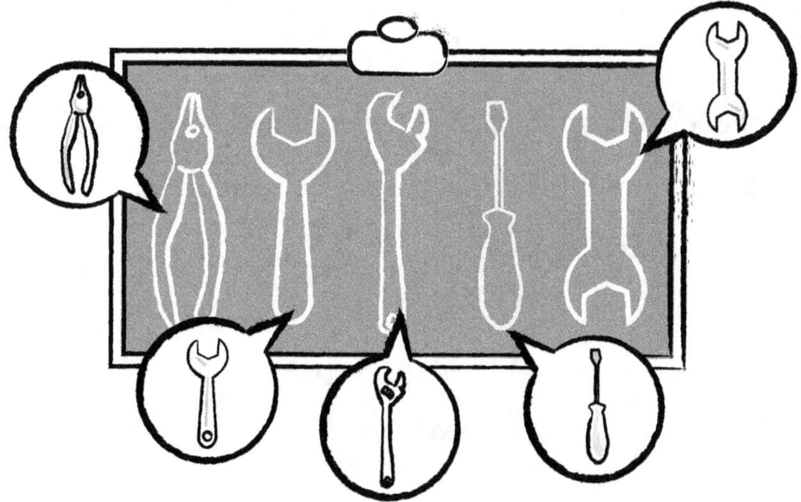

- To facilitate the location of items, identify items that are needed to make a particular product or job by a single color and store them in places painted the same color.

## How many items are there?

In the Selection stage (Seiri), we define the article's amount in our work area.

The identification of the reorder points as well as the maximum and minimum inventory levels gets simplified by marking them with a specific color:

- Maximum quantity – Red
- Minimum quantity – Yellow

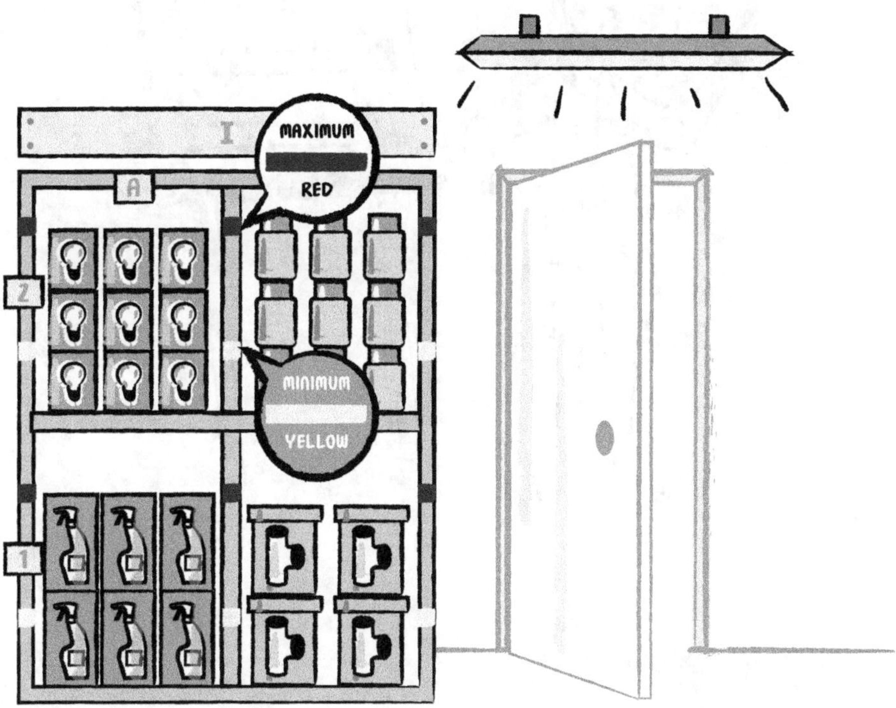



Everyone must know how you organize your work area; therefore, we must:

* Document the method of organization.
* Train people to follow procedures.

## CHAPTER SUMMARY

At the end of this stage, you'll see that the benefits include:

* More efficient use of resources by quickly locating what you need.
* Fewer accidents due to having visual aids.
* Fewer mistakes in the use of parts.

# Remember that Seiton (organize) is:

*"A place for everything,
and everything in its place"*

# Seiso (Shine)

Look carefully at the floors, hallways, and existing equipment in your work area. Have you ever wondered:

The amount of dust, dirt, or oil found?
And how about spotlights, lamps, windows, or behind cabinets and desks?

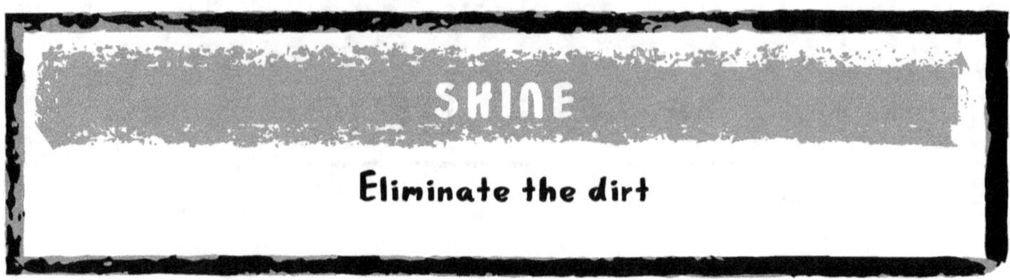


Cleaning our equipment and facilities helps us keep them in good condition and allows for a better use of our resources.

## CLEANING PROCESS

To keep the workplace in good condition, we must do the following.

To begin, we must ask ourselves:

## *What should we clean?*

| | |
|---|---|
| **Work area** | **Raw material warehouse, finished product, work in progress, replacement parts, etc.** |
| **Equipment** | **Machinery, tools, testing equipment.** |
| **Common Areas** | **Walkways, ceilings, walls, windows, bathrooms, lunchrooms, lamps, etc.** |

A practical way to organize cleaning activities is to draw a map of the entire work area into manageable locations and place a copy at each entrance zone.

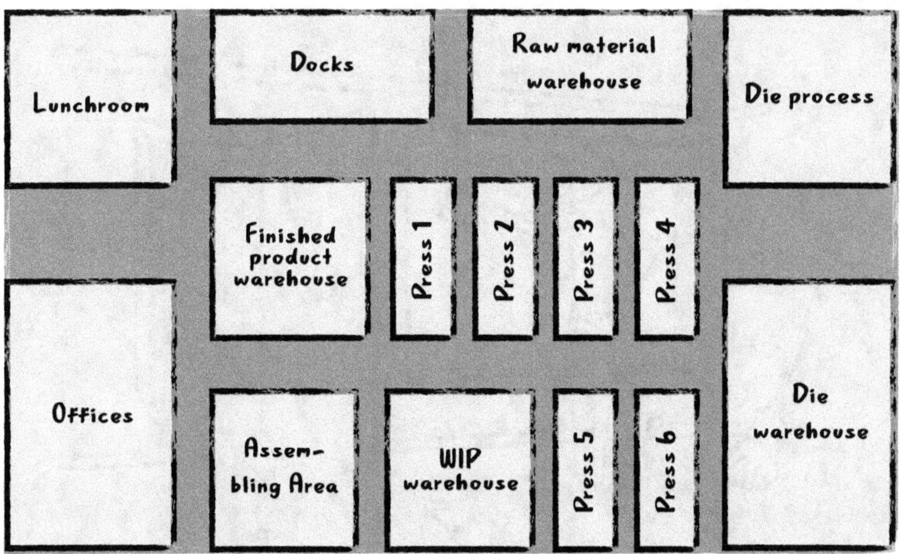

We must define what to clean, its frequency, how, and who should be responsible for cleaning activities.

Once this information is collected, we can document our cleaning program.

| CLEANING PROGRAM | | | | |
|---|---|---|---|---|
| Area | Articles | Responsible | Turn | Frequency |
| | Floor | W. Jones | 1st. | Daily |
| Press | Press | D. Evans | 2nd. | Weekly |
| #1 | Lamps | E. Thomas | 3rd. | Weekly |
| | Transporter | A. Taylor | 2nd. | Daily |

When assigning cleaning activities, keep in mind that the workers' responsibility is to keep their work area clean.

Once we have defined what to clean, when to clean, and who will do it, we need to establish how we'll do this activity.

▶ List each cleaning activity.

> **ACTIVITIES**
> 1. Clean packaging area.
> 2. Rinse bowls.
> 3. Clean transporters.
> 4. Sweep floors.

▶ List the cleaning supplies and equipment needed.

▶ Define a cleaning procedure.

> **REQUIRED EQUIPMENT**
> 1. Detergent.
> 2. Hose.
> 3. Cloth.
> 4. Broom.

> **CLEANING PROCEDURE**
>
> 1. Remove guards.
> 2. Clean windows.
> 3. Rinse the valves with water.
> 4. Put guards back.

## STEP 3: CREATE DISCIPLINE

All the effort and time invested up to this moment can be thrown to waste if the activities and discipline, defined in our 5S project, are not carried out daily.

When implementing the cleaning program, it's essential to provide all personnel involved with proper training and clear information to understand the how, the what, and the why to clean.

## To communicate

A way to encourage cleaning to become a habit is by informing each work area's peronnel of the expectations required of them.

To achieve this, we can place the map of our work area on a blackboard accompanied by the cleaning program and the cleaning procedures manual.

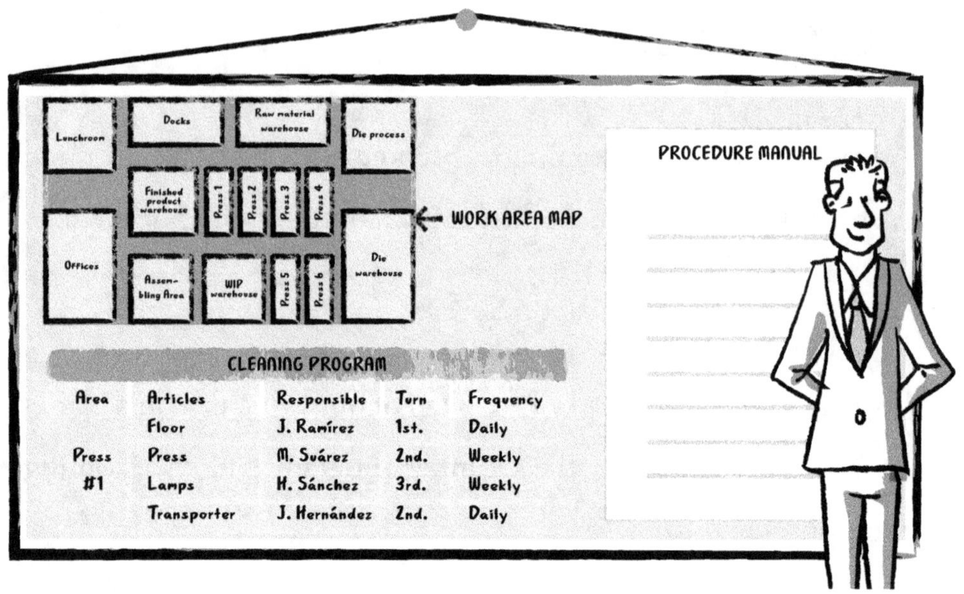




## Training

During training, we must ensure that the cleaning procedures are carried out down to the specific detail.

Other than this, monitoring is also an effective tool. In order to move forward, it is necessary to verify that the programmed activities are carried out and that we remove barrier to progress.

## CHAPTER SUMMARY

Working in a place where cleanliness is a standard of conduct provides us with advantages such as:

- Longer lasting equipment and machinery.
- Reduction of interruptions due to equipment and machinery failures.
- Lower accident rate.
- Better work environment.

Remember that for Seiso (Clean); we must understand that:

## CHAPTER 4

# Seiketsu (Standardize)

How many times have we finished our days' work, and everything looks flawless, but the next day we encounter an unpleasant surprise.

All the efforts invested so far can fall apart if discipline and the activities defined in our 5S project are not done routinely.

Ensure that procedures, practices, and activities are implemented consistently and on a regular basis. Ensure that Sort, Straighten, and Shine stages are maintained in the work areas.

There are two steps that we must follow:

## STEP 1: INTEGRATE THE 5S ACTIVITIES AT THE REGULAR WORK

There are several ways in which we can integrate the 5S activities into our daily work routines.

- We establish procedures. We document the activities we're setting and integrate these procedures into our work systems.

- Implement review audits. The sustained results of the first 3's put into action in our work areas must be verified. For the establishment of an adequate program of audits of the 5S, we must:

▶ Form a small group of auditors.

▶ Generate a checklist to determine the level of compliance in each work area.

▶ Develop an audit program. The recommendation is a monthly audit by area.

"WHAT'S NOT MEASURED CANNOT BE CONTROLLED, AND WHAT'S NOT CONTROLLED CANNOT BE IMPROVED."

Use the audits' results to quantitatively assess the level of implementation of the 5S in each work area.

Add an evaluation column to the verification list so that, according to the defined criteria, the degree of compliance achieved in the specific element evaluated gets graded.

| Element | # | Criteria | 1 | 2 | 3 | 4 | 5 |
|---|---|---|---|---|---|---|---|
| Organize | 1 | There are signs to identify the different areas and sub areas. | | | | X | |
| | 2 | The work areas, machinery, and equipment are clearly marked. | | | X | | |
| | 3 | All shelves and storage items are clearly identified. | | X | | | |
| | 4 | Visible identification that mark minimum and maximum storage levels are present. | X | | | | |

Don't forget to graph the results of the audits of each area.

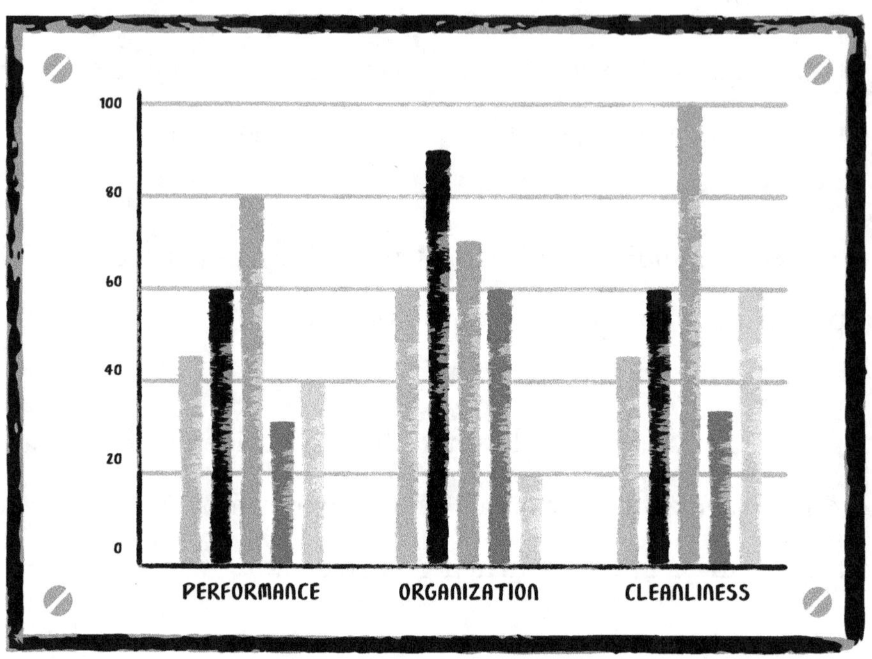



## PREVENTION

The best way to maintain results is by taking preventive measures in each of the first three "S".

- SELECT. Find methods to avoid the accumulation of unnecessary objects. The key is to control access of items that enter your work area.

- **ORGANIZE.** Avoid misplacing items. This will eliminate the need to return an article to its place of origin.

- **CLEAN.** We must avoid dirt in our work areas, and the key is to contain, or if possible, eliminate the source generating the dirt.

The great benefit obtained by standardizing our activities is to maintain the previous three "S" results in our work area.

Remember that Seiketsu (standardize) is:

# Shitsuke (Sustain)

One of the most powerful tools an administrator has is to verify the activities planned.

Verification will allow for a timely elimination of any barrier in order to achieve your goals. In other words, it allows you to follow up.

To create a culture in our organization, we must all actively participate. Everyone who collaborates in our work area must:

In order for people to know what the 5S are we must:

- Provide all company personnel with 5S training and make this course an essential requirement in the training program for new staff.
- Unfold the 5S program using:

▶ Posters

▶ Slogans

▶ Brochures

To encourage an enthusiastic participation of people in the 5S program, we must:

- Create recognition programs.
- Set an example with the involvement of the administration in projects and campaigns for 5S.
- Form teams to implement 5S projects in work areas.

To ensure that people participating in 5S projects have the necessary resources to work, we must do the following:

- Define and publicize the organizational structure that supports teams.
- Create communication channels between management and teams working on 5S projects.

▶ Presentation of projects by the teams to management.
▶ Periodic monitoring meetings between management and team leaders.

It is important to follow up on projects to avoid fleeting initiatives without affecting organizational permanence.

In order to achieve this, it is management's essential commitment as well as defined mechanisms that will promote knowledge in the 5S. Also, the foundations upon which a successful 5S program is built, is through the encouragement of motivational programs and providing the necessary resources to be functional.

Remember, for Shitsuke (Follow Up):

# Project Management

Once we know the meaning of each one of the 5S, we need to put them into practice.

How do we start?

These are the steps we suggest in implementing a 5S project in your area.

In these types of projects, teamwork is the best option because it favors human relationships, promotes creativity, and allows sharing activities among various people.

If possible, try to form natural teams, which are teams made up of members from the same work area.

**5S LEDGER**

**Name of the team:** Suits

**Area:** Testing lab

| Name | Role |
| --- | --- |
| Luis Socconini | Leader |
| Marco Barrantes | Member |
| Marcela Rodríguez | Member |
| Lorena Espinosa | Member |
| Sergio García | Member |
|  | Member |
|  | Member |
|  | Member |
|  | Member |

| | |
| --- | --- |
| Rubén Cárdenas | Facilitator |

**Date:** 28 december 2020

The team must designate a leader who, aside from actively participating like the rest of the members, assumes the responsibility and commitment to:

- Coordinate the work meetings.
- Represent the team in follow-up meetings with the facilitator.
- Document the results.

<table>
<tr><td colspan="3" align="center">TEAM AGENDA</td></tr>
</table>

**Objectives:**

1. Define dates and logistics to give 5S training.
2. Gather materials for preparation phase.
3

| Logistics: | | Members: | | |
|---|---|---|---|---|
| Date: | January 30, de 2020 | 1 | Luis Socconini | (Leader) |
| Hour: | 12:30 | 2 | Marco Barrantes | (Moderator) |
| Place: | Main room | 3 | Marcela Rodríguez | (Secretary) |
| Bring: | Date proposals | 4 | Lorena Espinosa | |
| | | 5 | Sergio García | |
| | | 6 | | |
| | | 7 | | |
| | | 8 | | |

**Agreements**

| Activity | Responsible | Dates |
|---|---|---|
| | | |
| | | |
| | | |
| | | |
| | | |

On the other hand, the role of a facilitator is just as important; usually, this is a person who has more authority within the organization and does not actively participate with work teams, however, takes care of:

- Providing resources to the team.
- Eliminating barriers that stand in the way of the group.
- Follow up on team performance.

Participants must know teamwork techniques to achieve better integration and an understanding of the 5S system.

- Teamwork.

  ▶ Integration of teams.
  ▶ Techniques for group decision-making.

- 5S system.

Divide this step into the following stages:

### Preparation stage

We recommend doing the following before identifying areas of opportunity:

- Take photos of your work area before and after the project to evaluate the changes generated.
- Identify the quarantined area (to store unnecessary objects).
- Prepare enough red cards to identify unnecessary objects.
- Get yellow cards or self-adhesive labels (Post-it) to write down ideas that will generate improvements in the area.

# Detection stage of opportunity areas

The time when team members identify activities in their work area for the following:

- Selection (place red cards).

| RED SLIP | | | |
|---|---|---|---|
| Date | 08/01/2020 | **Invoice** | 136 |
| Description | Personal computer (GDL1QC014) | | |
| Responsible | Sergio García | | |
| Date | 08/01/2020 | **Invoice** | 136 |
| Description | Personal computer (GDL1QC014) | | |
| **CATEGORY** | | | |
| Tools | | | |
| Buckets and containers | | | |
| Office equipment | | | X |
| Measurement tools | | | |
| Bbooks and papers | | | |
| Machinery | | | |
| Raw material | | | |
| Packing material | | | |
| Finished product | | | |
| WIP | | | |
| Spare parts | | | |
| Others | | | |
| **REASON** | | | |
| Contaminant | | | |
| Defected | | | |
| Broken | | | |
| Waste | | | |
| Not needed | | | X |
| Not needed soon | | | |
| Unknown use | | | |
| Other | | | |
| | | | |
| Responsible | Rubén Cárdenas | | |
| Decision date | 15/01/2020 | | |
| Final destination | | | |
| Date | | | |

- Organization (write down ideas on a post-it).

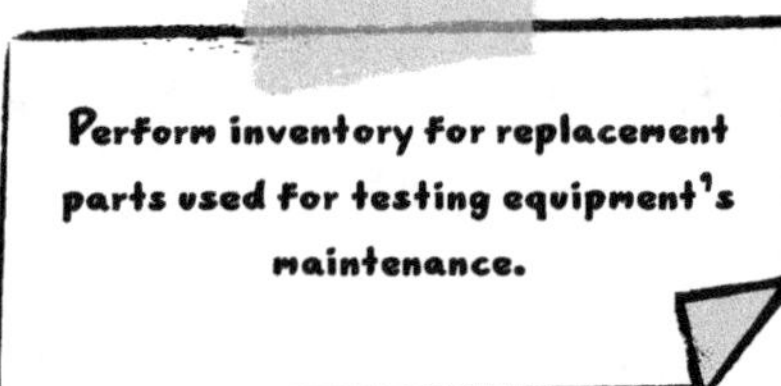



- Cleaning (jotting down ideas on a post-it).

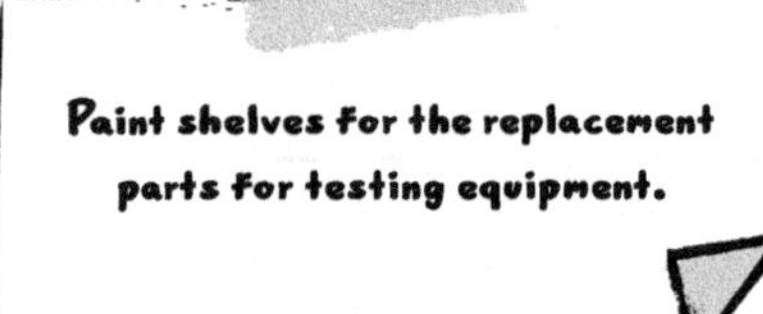



- Improvement (write down ideas on orange cards or post-it).

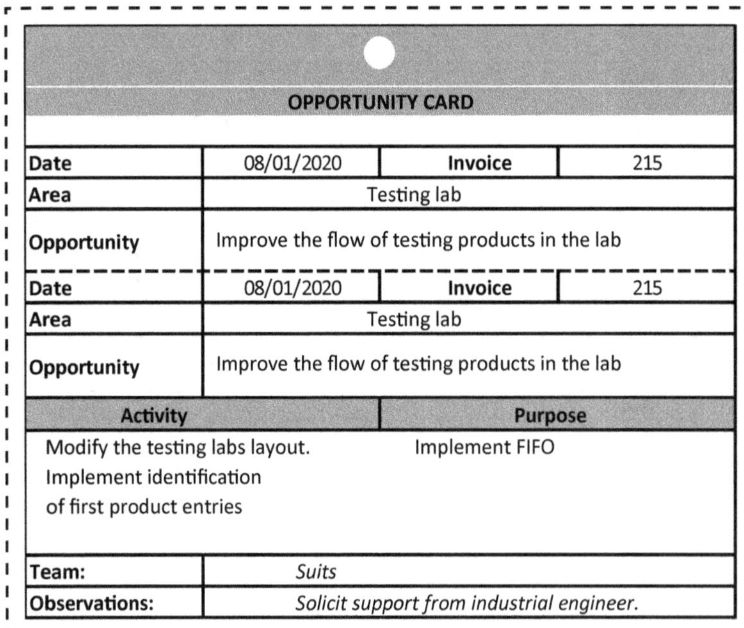

|  | OPPORTUNITY CARD | | |
|---|---|---|---|
| Date | 08/01/2020 | **Invoice** | 215 |
| Area | Testing lab | | |
| Opportunity | Improve the flow of testing products in the lab | | |
| Date | 08/01/2020 | **Invoice** | 215 |
| Area | Testing lab | | |
| Opportunity | Improve the flow of testing products in the lab | | |
| **Activity** | | **Purpose** | |
| Modify the testing labs layout. Implement identification of first product entries | | Implement FIFO | |
| Team: | *Suits* | | |
| Observations: | *Solicit support from industrial engineer.* | | |

It is suggested that the team first write down ideas and actions on a blackboard to:

- Eliminate repetition.
- Clarify what's confusing.
- Classify them in activities of selection, organization, cleaning, or improvement, according to the category to which they belong.

Organize the activities according to the time available to carry them out.

- TYPE A — Short-term type (1 to 2 weeks).
- TYPE B — Medium-term (3 to 4 weeks).
- TYPE C — Long term (1 to 2 months).

With this information, the team is ready to generate a report of the first 3's activities.

| 5S ACTIVITY REPORT | | | | |
|---|---|---|---|---|
| **Team:** | Suits | | | |
| **Area:** | Test laboratory | | | |
| **Invoice** | **Activity** | **Category** | **Deadline** | **Status** |
| 136 | Provide computer. | Selection | B | |
| N/A | Make inventory of spare parts used to maintain test equipment. | Organization | B | |
| N/A | Label standards to calibrate test equipment. | Organization | A | |
| N/A | Paint the shelf for spare parts of test equipment. | Cleaning | B | |
| N/A | Dust off computers and backs of work tables. | Cleaning | A | |
| 215 | Modify the lay-out of the laboratory and implement identification of first product entries. | To improve | C | |
| | | | | |

**Category:** Selection, Organization, Cleaning, Improvement.
**Deadline:** A (Short), B (Medium), C (Length).

The recommendation is to stick this sheet in the work area as a reminder of the upcoming activities.

Next, we must carry out the activities that we have scheduled.

As defined in our 5S project, the first activities to complete are selection and organization. These generally are done once, yet cleaning activities are done periodically.

At this stage, it is convenient to sort out cleaning activities and classify them accordingly, whether daily, weekly, or monthly. Then, document them into procedures to generate a cleaning schedule.

**CLEANING PROGRAM**

**Workplace:** *Testing lab*

| Area | Sub area | Responsible | Turn | Frequency |
|---|---|---|---|---|
| Common use | *Floors* | *W. Jones* | *1* | *Daily* |
| | *PC* | *D. Evans* | *2* | *Weekly* |
| | *Lamps* | *E. Thomas* | *3* | *Biweekly* |
| | *Shelves* | *A. Taylor* | *2* | *Biweekly* |
| | *Desks* | *R. Johnson* | *1* | *Daily* |
| Metrology | *Coordinates table* | *T. Williams* | *2* | *Weekly* |
| | *Viscometer* | *A. Miller* | *3* | *Daily* |
| | *Torquemeter* | *J. Davis* | *1* | *Daily* |
| | *Scale* | *M. Wilson* | *2* | *Weekly* |
| | | | | |

When we have completed at least 80% of the scheduled activities, it's recommended to retake the work area photos. At the beginning of the project, use the images taken as a reference and try and recreate the same positions and angles; thus, the improvements will be more evident.

Prepare a presentation with a summary of the activities carried out by the team, the results achieved, and the benefits obtained in the workplace.

During the presentation, the facilitator must ensure that upper management attends. This strengthens the message to employees regarding the commitment and active participation of the company's administration in the 5S initiative as well as stimulating team members.

## STEP 6: DO FOLLOW-UP AUDITS

Even if the project is not 100% finished, it's time to include our work area into our audit program.

| | | 5'S AUDIT | | | | | |
|---|---|---|---|---|---|---|---|

| Area of interest: | Testing lab | | | | | |
|---|---|---|---|---|---|---|
| Auditor: | Carlos Martinez | | | | Date: | 07/12/2020 |

| 5'S | Description to evaluate | Score | | | | |
|---|---|---|---|---|---|---|
| | | 1 | 2 | 3 | 4 | 5 |
| Select | 1. Can you find all necessary tools? | | | X | | |
| Select | 2. Can you only find materials that are needed? | | X | | | |
| Select | 3. Are the needed equipment's and materials separated correctly? | | X | | | |
| Straighten | 4. Is there a place for everything and everything in its place? | | | X | | |
| Straighten | 5. Are boundaries clearly marked with tape? | | | | X | |
| Straighten | 6. Is every tool labeled? | | | X | | |
| Shine | 7. Is the area clear of any objects or papers? | | | X | | |
| Shine | 8. Is the work furniture clean? | | | | X | |
| Shine | 9. Are the tools and materials needed for tasks cleaned? | | | X | | |
| Standardize | 10. Are there procedures related to maintaining the 5's in the work area? | | X | | | |
| Standardize | 11. . Is there evidence of execution of the procedures related to 5S? | | X | | | |
| Standardize | 12. Do the layout and photos correctly reflect the work standard in the area? | | X | | | |
| Sustain | 13. Does each member of the team comply with the four previous rules? | | | X | | |
| Sustain | 14. Is compliance with the 5S in constant improvement? | | | X | | |
| Sustain | 15. Does everyone you ask understand what the 5S consists of? | | | | X | |
| | TOTAL | 0 | 10 | 21 | 12 | 0 |

(1) Deficient. Nothing was done on this concept.
(2) Regular. Indications that it is necessary to work with greater effort.
(3) Good. There are areas or aspects to improve.
(4) Very well. With some sign of not being 100% finished.
(5) Excellent. The standards established for the 5'S are met.

Result: 57%
(Total amount / 75) x 100

First, we must complete the activities mentioned in the standardization stage (chapter 4) concerning the implementation of follow-up audits.

At the beginning of the project, we recommend to schedule audits weekly or fortnightly in the work area. Once we achieve better results, we can gradually reduce the frequency of these audits.

## STEP 7: REVIEW THE RESULTS

Each team must have in a visible place within the work area, the results obtained in the follow-up audits, their cleaning and activity schedules, and, if possible, photos showing how your working area should look.

This information will allow an easier approach for the team to continue managing their project and determining what new steps they need to implement. As a result, this allows one to keep in mind the feedback received from the follow-up audits and allows one to pursue progress in their work area.

# Paradigms

You'll probably face some common paradigms that interfere with the successful development of your 5S project, such as:

## LEADERSHIP PARADIGMS

**1.** The production equipment must not stop

The administration, faced with constant product delivery pressures, does not readily accept that a work area will be more productive when kept impeccable, neat, and clean. It considers cleaning a time-consuming task but fails to appreciate the benefits obtained by eliminating the causes of breakdowns, such as dust, lubrication in excess (excess oil), and other contamination sources.

**2.** Workers don't take care of things

Workers are sure to appreciate the benefits because they're the ones who are directly affected by the lack of 5S implements.

**3.** There Are several expedite orders to waste time cleaning

It's easy to neglect order and cleanliness when there's an urgent need for work to be done. Occasionally other activities have to wait; however, 5S actions should be seen as an investment to achieve all requests in the future and not only the ones needed for the present.

**4.** The current state is adequate. We don't need the 5S

Some consider that only the visible aesthetics of the equipment are sufficient. However, the 5S serve to identify equipment problems since it's the operator's contact with the machine which allows identifying breakdowns that can turn into big problems. Cleaning must be the first stage in the preventive maintenance inspection at the plant.

1. I am paid to work, not to clean

   Sometimes the staff accepts dirt as an unavoidable condition of their workstation. The worker is not aware of the negative effect a dirty workplace has on their safety, quality of work, and productivity.

2. I don't see the need to apply the 5S

   It can be challenging to implement the 5S in companies that are very efficient or very clean. However, not everything has to do with removing dust or contamination. The 5S improve the equipment's visual control, safety for the people operating the machines, and employees' active participation.

# Trend Technologies

## PLANT GUADALAJARA SOUTH

### Company description

Founded in 2000 in Guadalajara, the plant Trend Technologies, Inc. began operations of manufacturing and marketing stamped parts for the electronics industry. It has a strong presence at the regional level selling its products to the leading maquiladora companies, including Flextronics, Solectron, Jabil, and Sanmina.

Trend Technologies has design and manufacturing processes of molds and dies, injection of plastic parts, die-cutting mechanical components, mechanical assemblies, and electrostatic painting. These processes allow the company to offer integral solutions to develop new products in relatively short periods of time.

## Background

In 1999 the plant began operations as Cowden Metal. Its facilities were built on 150,000 square feet, with state-of-the-art technology to ensure metal parts' production with the quality demanded by the electronics industry standards.

In 2003, Trend Technologies bought Cowden Metal Guadalajara to add the stamping metal process to their plastic injection operation. This strategic maneuver positioned the company as one of the few in the region to offer comprehensive solutions for the assembly of electronic items to the large maquiladoras in Guadalajara's metropolitan area.

## Problem

As a result of its strategic plan to increase sales, Trend Technologies plant Guadalajara decides to enter the automotive market to expand its customer base.

A requirement to be a direct or indirect supplier to most automobile assembly companies in Mexico is the ISO/TS 16949 standard. This standard establishes the quality management system requirements for the design, development, and production of products and services related to the automotive industry. Thus, certifying its quality system under the ISO / TS 16949 standard becomes a priority for Trend Technologies.

In addition to entering new markets, the organization knows the need to be more productive and lower costs. Hence, it decides to implement an efficient manufacturing system under the Lean Manufacturing philosophy.

To support both initiatives, Trend Technologies understands the need to improve the organization, cleanliness, safety, and discipline of their work areas. Consequently, it decides to implement the 5S in its manufacturing plant.

## The 5S project

The objectives sought by the organization with this project are: improve the organization, safety, and cleanliness of their work areas, increase productivity, improve quality, reduce waste, identify operational problems, as well as facilitate the access and return of articles between the production areas and their warehouses.

Trend Technologies named their project SOLES for the initials of the words (Spanish):

- Select (seleccionar)

- Organize (organizar)

- Clean (limpiar)

- Standardize (estandarizar)

- Maintain (sostener)

First, they gathered a team made up of the various departments' managers to define the plan to implement the 5S. An appointed quality manager gave all organization staff talks about the SOLES program's purpose and content. These first talks helped them understand the program's basics and communicate the importance of this program for the organization, allowing them to create the necessary insight for the staff to accept changes in their work.

With all organization members' enthusiastic participation, the implementation of selection, organization, and cleaning began.

Sustaining, commonly the most challenging stage to achieve when implementing the 5S, was quickly assimilated in Trend thanks to management's active participation. They included the status review of their work areas as part of their daily tours, took immediate action to correct deviations, and provided direct feedback to their staff. Order, cleanliness, and discipline are now established working routines in the company.

Trend Technologies managed to certify its quality system under ISO / TS 16949 standard and currently manufactures parts for direct suppliers of assembly factories of the automotive industry.

As part of the strategy to develop a lean manufacturing system, Kanban cards' implementation had made it possible to reduce the inventories of raw materials, product in-process, and finished product.

The company is currently looking to implement a Six Sigma program under the DMAIC methodology to apply statistical and administrative tools to improve the company's processes and products and increase its customers' satisfaction.

## Reflections - Conclusions

The involvement and active participation of management was fundamental in the successful implementation of the SOLES program. This program has been an excellent platform to support its continuous process of quality and productivity improvement.

The Trend Technologies director's vision has improved its position to face the current market's competitiveness.

# Verde Valle Products

## PLANT GUADALAJARA

### Company Description

Productos Verde Valle, S.A. de C.V. is a company dedicated to the processing, distribution, marketing, and researching of healthy food products with aggregate value.

### Background

Founded in 1967, the company has headquarters in Guadalajara, Jalisco, Mexico. Also, with divisions in Monterrey, Mexico City, Tijuana, and Dallas, Texas. Green Valley has maintained a strategic partnership with ConAgra Foods since 1996.

Productos Verde Valle initiated a 5S implementation project to improve all its production processes.

The organization's objectives with this project were: supporting good manufacturing practices, aligning the project to the needs of HACCP certification (hygiene and safety), improving working areas, increasing productivity, and improving its quality.

The quality manager, Ing. Verónica Estrada, heads this project, who had initially taught training courses for all staff on good manufacturing practices and the correct application of the 5S.

Initially, it represented a great challenge for them; they started getting the staff ready by teaching courses and creating an internal video to communicate the 5S program.

The project began by choosing a pilot area. They picked cereals, making sure that hygiene and quality were top priority.

They obtained favorable results in the order and selection steps. They noticed the possibility of reducing their processes' inventories and having a visual factory with better space use.

They formed four teams to carry out this task, each with a leader and a firm commitment to achieving comprehensive results.

Each team received training to apply the 5S in their work areas and to express ideas that would develop, in many cases, into actions that would help improve the presentation of their working spaces. Later, they realized that cleaning was not only for exterior spaces but also for knowing their equipment and taking better care of it.

The cleaning phase represented a significant achievement, not just concerning the cleaning aspect. It also helps find hidden problems and highlights relevant things to improve (for example, mechanical parts equipment that requires lubrication, not often noticed). It's essential to perform operator-specific routines in which they do simple but functional maintenance to the equipment.

According to official norms and safety signaling, the standardization stage defined color codes like the lines' thickness, the machines' color, and a signaling type, both for devices and the pipe colors.

This step was of great importance since it allowed other areas to use it as a reference to systemize and provide follow-up on successive implementations.

## Results

Finally, each team documented these achievements and the complete implementation process and presented it to the CEO and president of the company, who dedicated time to listen directly to their experiences and expressed the following conclusions:

- Better performance of processes in efficiency and quality.

- Better understanding and communication between staff, since they had the opportunity to work as a team and meet.

- Better hygiene and safety in your processes.

- Better visual aspect of the facilities.

- Support for manufacturing practices.

- Appreciation from supervisors and managers for the valuable work in support of the company.

# Luminosos Correa

## Company Description

Luminosos Correa is a Chilean company that manufactures illuminated informational advertisements. Within a continuous improvement process, given the implementation of lean manufacturing, it decided to put the 5S methodology into practice to improve operations.

## Background

Luminosos Correa is a family business, with its parent company in Chile, in Temuco in the Araucanía region. Since its inception in 1972, it has dedicated itself to produce various informational and advertising signs. Thanks to technological advances and a constant effort in training its workers, it guarantees quality safety products and services.

The company has three departments that constitute the business units: Electronics, metallic structures, and road signs & advertising, each in charge of their production processes, marketing, research and development. It also has a General Services department in charge of administrative, financial, and logistical support for each business unit.

## Problem

For the Metallic Structures area, the decision made was to implement the 5S methodology to maintain order and efficient follow-up of customer orders and ensure constant and consistent quality. The director of this area, engineer Patricio Correa, expresses their intention to create its quality system based on ISO 9000 and the 5S as pillars of standardization and daily activities to develop a solid business culture.

Another purpose of the project was the employees' safety; by having clean, orderly, and standardized facilities, they'd achieve greater safety for their staff; therefore, this aspect was a priority.

First, they carried out an internal marketing campaign to promote and inform staff of this Japanese methodology used in many countries with proven success. They prepared the employees to know the method by using a comparison viewpoint with the best (benchmarking), highlighting results, and proposing ways to adapt this tool to a different culture, always with the commitment to improve.

Among the fundamental activities carried out at the beginning of the project was recording the various areas' conditions through photographs. Then placing them on communication boards, corridors, and dining rooms, to highlight their current state and make the staff think of this as the starting point of a race with a finish line called 5S.

They established a pilot implementation committee consisting of the director, four workers, two maintenance mechanics, and a person responsible for the human resources department to carry out this project. This team learned the basics of the methodology for its correct application.

Later, they carried out tests to verify that the equipment was ready. Once verified, they carried out the training of the rest of the personnel. They divided the staff into seven teams; its members chose a name and a color for each group. To symbolize the competition, they represented each team with a horse of the corresponding color and then pasted the image in a clear view to simulate a horse race. The finish line being short-term goals representing the implementation stages, thus monitoring each team's progress.

The race began with a symbolic starting flag given by its leader, the engineer Correa, who explains the great enthusiasm aroused by this project; this was the main ingredient of any project since motivation accomplishes more than effort alone.

At the beginning of the implementation, they had interesting experiences. When selecting what was helpful from what was not, they were able to gather so many objects; they organized a bazaar from things that were too big and years unused, getting a windfall profit at the time.

The different teams wanted each to impose a distinctive strategy at organizing and make their implementation differ from the other groups in the ordering stage.

Creativity was a significant and decisive factor since the implicit search for improvement opportunities was also a significant step in implementing ISO 9000. It was a success to combine them and not have isolated victories since both the 5S and the ISO 9000 system are the pillars of its culture.

Once the cleaning stage started, teams began to separate; the horse's advances were notorious because some tasks were dirtier and messier than others. Seeing the horses spread out and feeling surpassed, groups saw themselves in a constant competition that worked as an engine for the implementation.

It's important to emphasize that many things were common to all during the implementation in different areas, such as having unnecessary objects, needless saved documents, defects hiding in the garbage due to the lack of order.

Ultimately, the teams that finished their projects and were winners became an aid to their colleagues who, due to lack of time, overwork, and sometimes lack of motivation, did not finish; it promoted camaraderie and proved the seriousness of this project.

With the information and photographs collected during implementation, each team leader presented their experiences to the director. The presentation mentioned the obstacles as well as the achievements obtained. It emphasized the sense of fellowship and the opportunity to work as a team, allowing them to know each other and feel more valuable. Being able to contribute ideas and have them taken into account had been of great value.

## Results

Among the outstanding results of the implementation, we can mention the following:

* Motivation of staff in their work.

- More and better fellowship.

- Less time searching for tools and materials.

- Better follow-up of customer orders.

- Better quality of products.

## Reflections - Conclusions

Management participation in implementing this project was relevant since it denotes a substantial commitment of support and involvement; the staff's enthusiasm also made this a formidable experience in achieving its goals.

# Cueros del Fin del Mundo

## (Leather from the edge of the world)

## Company Description

Cueros del Fin del Mundo is an Argentine company that manufactures and sells leather goods, conducting a business transformation towards a culture of quality and high performance, implementing the 5S system in its warehouse spare parts and dies to maintain order and control.

## Background

Cueros del Fin del Mundo, S.A. started its operations in 1998 in Buenos Aires, Argentina, as an innovative company producing leather goods with prints made with a laser beam, allowing unique designs according to customer needs. It started with only three workers, but little by little, it has grown, and to date, 25 employees work in different areas: marketing, sales, administration, production, and distribution.

This company has developed thanks to the growing demand for Argentine leather products and the distinction of being a company introducing laser engraving, making it the most successful in this technology applied to the leather industry.

## Problem

To stay at the forefront of technology, Cueros del Fin del Mundo, S.A., has decided to apply the 5S methodology to improve warehouse management, stop losing tools, and have the necessary spare parts always available.

Previously they had the problem of handling tools without any control and in different places, then lost by not returning them to the warehouse. When they needed to repair a machine production required to deliver the orders placed, they wasted time looking for them because they had no set place.

## 5S project

Its director and principal shareholder, Mariano Posbeyikian, decided to implement the methodology after learning about it thanks to a course received on its application and benefits.

The project began with the company's personnel training to inform them about its benefits and application.

Mr. Posbeyikian said that workers were initially skeptical, since being a Japanese methodology, they believed it would be challenging to apply in an Argentine company. After seeing the ease of application and the power of its results, they decided to adopt it as a proven solution and incorporate it into the company's culture.

To begin and determine the company's current conditions, they took photographs of the spare parts warehouse and the repair shop.

## Interior of the spare parts warehouse

They placed the photographs mentioned before as notices in different meetinghouses, and everybody was able to see the deplorable state of order and cleanliness in such an important place.

The process began by separating all used spare parts without use, all the garbage and dust of the area, and removing everything that was not spare parts, dies, or maintenance materials.

The process had many problems because some materials were considered valid for some but garbage for others. Consequently, they designated two quarantine areas to hold them for a limited time of 30 days to sell or be used if needed.

In the next step, called "order," they conducted team activities to tidy up the warehouse; they formed a team with personnel from the maintenance, production, and quality departments. It was important to consider everyone with articles related to their department to be present in the selection and ordering process to avoid throwing away something or keeping it without need.

In the cleaning stage, called "super cleaning," the goal was not just to clean up but also to make the area look impeccable. The step started by painting walls, sealing the room so that no dust or particles from the process itself enter, and coating the floor with epoxy paint, giving it a flawless look.

This step was crucial for a "total" change of appearance of the area. From that moment on, the desired "impeccable warehouse" concept began to take effect; the staff received it well since they considered it part of their achievement.

They equipped the area with a computer and installed a program to carry the warehouse's inventory for better control. These changes took place due to the interest and professionalism exhibited at this stage and management's conviction that it was time to invest in modernizing that area. The progress and achievements until that moment motivated a renewal stage in the business.

The standardization stage's objective was to document everything done until this moment and began using the concepts, colors, times, materials, and the rest as a standard for other areas implementing the 5S. Also, to carry the necessary activities to keep these spaces the same or, if possible, improve them.

The standardization stage reinforcement used routines of well-defined activities executed by specific managers selected by either their position or responsibility. Anyone holding the position knew precisely this was a team responsibility and not a personalized action. They assigned specific tasks, even if personnel changed due to rotation.

## Results

The results speak for themselves, to mention a few:

- Total control of materials.
- Significant reduction in storage costs.
- A decrease in lost materials.
- All materials' disponibility allows a quick response to the client when preparing and delivering their orders before the deadline.
- Higher productivity by using less material and time in orders.
- Excellent order and control of warehouses.

Finally, the director explained that to bring this initiative to a lasting effect and make it into a plan of action that'll motivate employees, they had to evaluate the implementation's evolution weekly. Those appraising were people chosen at random so that everyone learned to locate and identify the aspects of having a clean and orderly area. In this initiative, each person had the chance to analyze the benefits, provide ideas at the end of the audit report, and envision it as the first stage of a successful implementation.

# Technicolor Mexicana

## PLANT GUADALAJARA

### Company Description

Technicolor México, Guadalajara plant, belongs to the corporate digital content solutions division Thomson. The company is mainly engaged in the manufacturing of DVDs for the film industry. Technicolor Mexico Guadalajara plant is the World's Largest manufacturing plant of DVD and Blue Ray. It manufactures movies for the most important cinematographic studio films, like Disney, Dreamworks, Universal, Paramount, Sony, Warner, Lions Gate, and more, in addition to video games for Microsoft's X-Box line.

The main competitive advantages of the company are:

* The largest optical disc manufacturer in the world.
* Member of a renowned global corporation.
* A leader in technology.
* A leader in the development of improvements in production.
* Very robust supply, manufacturing, and logistics processes.
* Mainly an exporting company.
* IRMA certification (International Recording Media Association) as a manufacturer that meets anti-piracy security requirements.

## Background

Technicolor Mexico is an organization that was born as the area of Kodak floppy disks from Mexico. Due to technological evolution, it switched to the manufacture of Recordable Compact Discs or RCD. Subsequently, Kodak and Panasonic decided to create a strategic alliance that resulted in the compact disc area becoming a separated from Kodak, forming what was known as Matsushita Media Export.

One of the main reasons for this alliance was the diversification of products; therefore, they decided to manufacture digital Videos or DVDs. At the time, it started with only four production lines to manufacture DVDs. Later, Thomson corporate chose to acquire the Panasonic area manufacturing  DVDs from Mexico and the one from the United States; it undid the strategic alliance of Kodak - Panasonic, and Technicolor Mexicana was born.

Technicolor Mexico currently has more than 1,000 employees, with an average age of fewer than 32 years, six months. The population composition is 57% men and 43% women.

## Problem

In a short period, Technicolor Mexico experienced explosive growth, increasing its installed capacity by 3,000%. The number of jobs created grew more than four times its staff number in just 19 months.

To fulfill its mission of "Providing its clients with optical discs fast, free of defects at the lowest cost in the world," Technicolor management defined "quality leadership" as one of its strategies. This strategy consists of developing fail-safe systems manufacturing practices. To ensure compliance with the client's requirements, the company defined a plan composed of the following elements:

1.  The understanding and incorporation of the needs of the client into our processes.
2.  Detailed knowledge of our processes.
3.  Identification of the failure modes of the product and the processes.
4.  The development of control systems.
5.  The development of practical operating procedures.
6.  Training, ongoing instruction, and our people's registration performance.
7.  Permanent verification of the status of our quality system, our processes, and our products.
8.  The application of a system ensures the implementation of controlled changes.
9.  The use of preventive, corrective, and improvement action systems.
10. The certification of its quality and environmental systems.
11. The permanent strengthening of our culture of quality.

The main project to permanently strengthen its culture quality (point number eleven of the leadership strategy in quality) is to implement a 5S program.

The program's objective is:

*Implementing the 5S in all production areas.*

The purpose of implementing the 5S program in Technicolor is that their work areas achieve the following characteristics:

1. Be neat and clean.
2. Be efficient.
3. Look professional.

The following explains in detail what it means for the company to achieve each of these characteristics:

Neat and clean work areas.

- Create the conditions for a pleasant workplace that contributes to improving satisfaction and our employees' quality of life.

Efficient work areas.

- Eliminate waste produced by disorder, lack of cleanliness, leaks, contamination, and more, and improve the work environment.

- Improve discipline in compliance with standards, with our staff's participation in preparing procedures for organizing and cleaning their work area.

- Use visual controls to keep order in the items and tools involved in the productive process.

- Preserve the work area and the company resources in the best possible condition by maintaining the improvements achieved when applying the first 3S.

Professional work areas.

- One of the chief purposes of implementing the 5S is that our factory is always impeccable, looking like a showroom, displaying the people visiting where and how we make our products. We know that people who know how we carry out our operations trust us more; thanks to this trust, our relationships are strengthened and, consequently, increases our business opportunities.

To implement the 5S program, Technicolor created a work team made up of people representing its different departments and the company's general direction as a sponsor.

To facilitate the team's work, gradually gain experience, and obtain short-term results, the decision was to start implementing the 5S in only one of the eight segments of the production area.

The following describes the work plan defined by Technicolor:

1. Creating the work team.
2. Training in the 5S methodology.
3. Identification of opportunities.
4. Standardization.
5. Audit process.
6. Results review.
7. General implementation plan throughout the plant.

## Results

Implementing improvement projects in the production area got extraordinary results with the 5S and other projects' help. The best efficiency in the execution of operations has been impacted in part because:

- Operators have better tools to perform their functions.

- No time wasted looking for tools and materials.

- The work area is more pleasant and safe.

- Staff is more motivated and engaged.

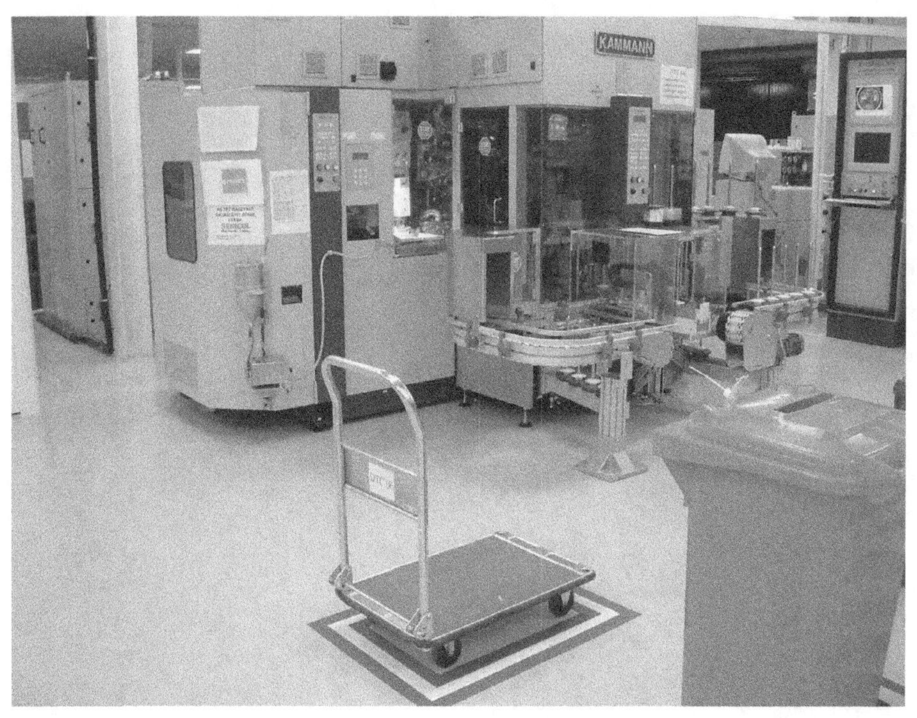

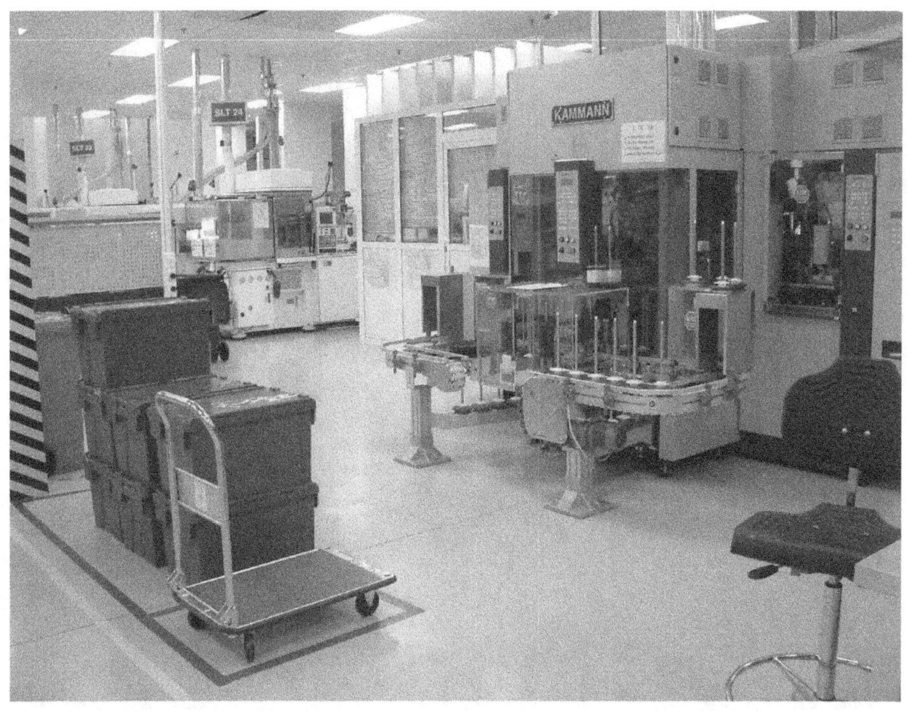

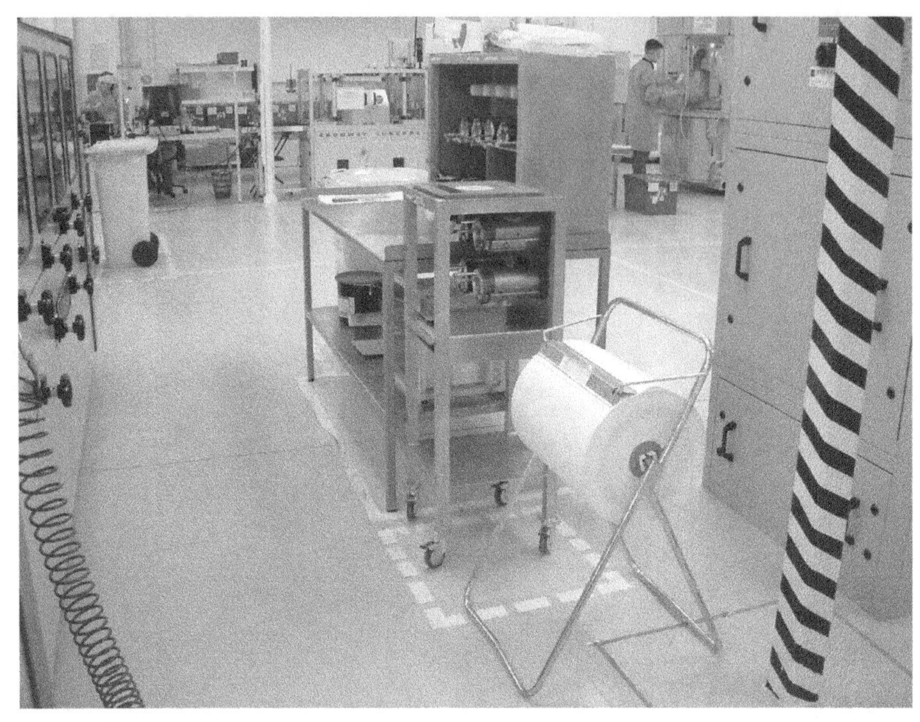

# BICO Internacional

## Company description

BICO Internacional is a Colombian company dedicated to producing and distributing consumer products in college school stationery, office, and staff.

BICO International offers students, professionals, and consumers of different ages a full range of essential products that help make communication more accessible and better manage information, creating more social and practical work. Since its inception, this company has been one of the leading paper converters in Colombia by manufacturing products such as notebooks, folders, blocks, accounting books, envelopes, carbon paper, paper rolls, diaries, folding paper, and wrapping paper.

This company carries out a process of continuous improvement that has led them to implement the 5S as part of the Total Productive Maintenance program.


## Background

In 1904, Mr. Manuel Carvajal Valencia, with his sons Alberto and Hernando Carvajal, began the CARVAJAL activities in a modest company focused on graphic arts.

The School Products division started activities around 45 years ago, intending to supply articles for school use.

In 1995 BICO International became one of the eight Carvajal Group companies, integrating Ofinorma, Datacar, Kiut, and School Products.

The implementation of the 5S, arises in BICO International with the adoption of the TPM improvement philosophy (Total Productive Maintenance) as a continuous improvement tool. This philosophy consists of the development of 8 Pillars, one of them the Autonomous Maintenance, focused on achieving that the equipment operator becomes the manager of its production process, being the owner and responsible for maintenance by inspection, cleaning, and lubrication.

The problems they faced before the implementation of the 5S:

- Unnecessary elements for the production process.
- Excessive filth on equipment and materials.
- Disorder of materials and tools.
- Unsafe work sites.
- Low morale in employees.
- A high number of stoppages of minor equipment.
- Loss of time changing formats.

## The 5S project

For the implementation, production managers learned to be trainers of the philosophy; then, they chose the crew and the pilot team to put into effect the program and acquire experience. The pilot team members received uniforms that identified them as the improvement group's elements, which generated positive expectations in the plant's other collaborators.

They trained the pilot group; they delivered the necessary elements for its implementation and took notes of the obstacles faced, documenting through photographs the achievements and progress made.

Later, with graphic materials' help, they displayed the information to the rest of the plant to announce the achievements and team progress.


## Results

Some of the benefits achieved in matters of order and cleanliness, as well as with their continuous maintenance, were:

- A high degree of motivation and commitment from the staff of the plant.
- Creation of a pleasant and safe working environment.
- Reduction of downtime in equipment.
- Reduction in the level of waste.

They maintained order and cleanliness:

- Through the creation of monthly spaces, where employees proudly present their bosses and colleagues with the most outstanding advances and improvement cases; this work receives recognition from the company.

The process and the results influenced the behavior and performance of people as follows:

- Through their 5S work, the collaborators appropriated the equipment, creating an affective bond, which prompted them to respect and have their workplaces respected.
- Employees began to experience a high level of motivation.
- Each improvement group managed to acquire an identity, enhance teamwork, and highlight the individual contribution to achieve the group's objectives.

# Conclusions

The 5S strategy is a simple concept often not given enough importance; however, an area of clean and safe work allows directing people towards the following goals:

- Respond to the need to improve the work environment and avoid waste caused by a disorder, lack of cleaning, leaks, contamination, and more.
- Reduce losses due to quality problems, delivery time response, and costs, with staff intervention in taking care of their workplace, ensuring a pleasant environment.
- Create the conditions to increase the equipment's useful life through permanent inspection by staff that operates the machinery.
- Improve standardization and discipline, and staff can participate in the development of cleaning procedures.
- Use of visual control elements. Like cards and boards, keep in order all the parts and tools that intervene in the production process.

- Maintain the workplace in optimal conditions by regular checks on maintenance actions of the improvements achieved with the application of the 5S.
- Reduce the potential causes of accidents, requiring an increased awareness of care and conservation of the company's equipment and other resources.
- Implement any quality and productivity improvement program, like Total Quality or Lean Manufacturing.

# Repeatable Formats

---

- Register of 5S projects.
- Team agenda.
- Red card.
- Opportunity card.
- Report of opportunities of the 5S.
- Cleaning program.
- Audit of the 5S.

**5S LEDGER**

| **Name of the team:** | Suits |
|---|---|
| **Area:** | Testing lab |

| Name | Role |
|---|---|
| Luis Socconini | Leader |
| Marco Barrantes | Member |
| Marcela Rodríguez | Member |
| Lorena Espinosa | Member |
| Sergio García | Member |
|  | Member |
|  | Member |
|  | Member |
|  | Member |

| Rubén Cárdenas | Facilitator |
|---|---|

| **Date:** | 28 december 2020 |
|---|---|

<table>
<tr><td colspan="3" align="center">TEAM AGENDA</td></tr>
</table>

**Objectives:**

1. Define dates and logistics to give 5S training.

2. Gather materials for preparation phase.

3 _______________________________________________

| Logistics: | |
|---|---|
| Date: | January 30, de 2020 |
| Hour: | 12:30 |
| Place: | Main room |
| Bring: | Date proposals |
| | |
| | |
| | |
| | |

| Members: | | |
|---|---|---|
| 1 | Luis Socconini | (Leader) |
| 2 | Marco Barrantes | (Moderator) |
| 3 | Marcela Rodríguez | (Secretary) |
| 4 | Lorena Espinosa | |
| 5 | Sergio García | |
| 6 | | |
| 7 | | |
| 8 | | |

**Agreements**

| Activity | Responsible | Dates |
|---|---|---|
| | | |
| | | |
| | | |
| | | |
| | | |

<table>
<tr><td colspan="4" align="center">○</td></tr>
<tr><td colspan="4" align="center">RED SLIP</td></tr>
<tr><td>Date</td><td>08/01/2020</td><td>Invoice</td><td>136</td></tr>
<tr><td>Description</td><td colspan="3" align="center">Personal computer (GDL1QC014)</td></tr>
<tr><td>Responsible</td><td colspan="3" align="center">Sergio García</td></tr>
<tr><td>Date</td><td>08/01/2020</td><td>Invoice</td><td>136</td></tr>
<tr><td>Description</td><td colspan="3" align="center">Personal computer (GDL1QC014)</td></tr>
</table>

| CATEGORY | |
|---|---|
| Tools | |
| Buckets and containers | |
| Office equipment | X |
| Measurement tools | |
| Bbooks and papers | |
| Machinery | |
| Raw material | |
| Packing material | |
| Finished product | |
| WIP | |
| Spare parts | |
| Others | |

| REASON | |
|---|---|
| Contaminant | |
| Defected | |
| Broken | |
| Waste | |
| Not needed | X |
| Not needed soon | |
| Unknown use | |
| Other | |

| | |
|---|---|
| Responsible | *Rubén Cárdenas* |
| Decision date | *15/01/2020* |
| Final destination | |
| Date | |

## OPPORTUNITY CARD

| Date | 08/01/2020 | Invoice | 215 |
|---|---|---|---|
| Area | Testing lab | | |
| Opportunity | Improve the flow of testing products in the lab | | |

| Date | 08/01/2020 | Invoice | 215 |
|---|---|---|---|
| Area | Testing lab | | |
| Opportunity | Improve the flow of testing products in the lab | | |

| Activity | Purpose |
|---|---|
| Modify the testing labs layout. Implement identification of first product entries | Implement FIFO |
| Team: | *Suits* |
| Observations: | *Solicit support from industrial engineer.* |

## 5S ACTIVITY REPORT

| Team: | *Suits* |
|---|---|
| Area: | *Test laboratory* |

| Invoice | Activity | Category | Deadline | Status |
|---|---|---|---|---|
| 136 | *Provide computer.* | *Selection* | *B* | |
| N/A | *Make inventory of spare parts used to maintain test equipment.* | *Organization* | *B* | |
| N/A | *Label standards to calibrate test equipment.* | *Organization* | *A* | |
| N/A | *Paint the shelf for spare parts of test equipment.* | *Cleaning* | *B* | |
| N/A | *Dust off computers and backs of work tables.* | *Cleaning* | *A* | |
| 215 | *Modify the lay-out of the laboratory and implement identification of first product entries.* | *To improve* | *C* | |
| | | | | |

**Category:** *Selection, Organization, Cleaning, Improvement.*

**Deadline:** *A (Short), B (Medium), C (Length).*

**CLEANING PROGRAM**

**Workplace:**        *Testing lab*

| Area | Sub area | Responsible | Turn | Frequency |
|---|---|---|---|---|
| Common use | *Floors* | *W. Jones* | *1* | *Daily* |
| | *PC* | *D. Evans* | *2* | *Weekly* |
| | *Lamps* | *E. Thomas* | *3* | *Biweekly* |
| | *Shelves* | *A. Taylor* | *2* | *Biweekly* |
| | *Desks* | *R. Johnson* | *1* | *Daily* |
| Metrology | *Coordinates table* | *T. Williams* | *2* | *Weekly* |
| | *Viscometer* | *A. Miller* | *3* | *Daily* |
| | *Torquemeter* | *J. Davis* | *1* | *Daily* |
| | *Scale* | *M. Wilson* | *2* | *Weekly* |
| | | | | |

<table>
<tr><td colspan="8" align="center">5´S AUDIT</td></tr>
<tr><td>Area of interest:</td><td colspan="7">Testing lab</td></tr>
<tr><td>Auditor:</td><td colspan="5">Carlos Martínez</td><td>Date:</td><td>07/12/2020</td></tr>
</table>

| 5´S | Description to evaluate | 1 | 2 | 3 | 4 | 5 |
|---|---|---|---|---|---|---|
| | | | | | | Score |
| **Select** | 1. Can you find all necessary tools? | | | X | | |
| | 2. Can you only find materials that are needed? | | X | | | |
| | 3. Are the needed equipment's and materials separated correctly? | | X | | | |
| **Straighten** | 4. Is there a place for everything and everything in its place? | | | X | | |
| | 5. Are boundaries clearly marked with tape? | | | | X | |
| | 6. Is every tool labeled? | | | X | | |
| **Shine** | 7. Is the area clear of any objects or papers? | | | X | | |
| | 8. Is the work furniture clean? | | | | X | |
| | 9. Are the tools and materials needed for tasks cleaned? | | | X | | |
| **Standardize** | 10. Are there procedures related to maintaining the 5's in the work area? | | X | | | |
| | 11. . Is there evidence of execution of the procedures related to 5S? | | X | | | |
| | 12. Do the layout and photos correctly reflect the work standard in the area? | | X | | | |
| **Sustain** | 13. Does each member of the team comply with the four previous rules? | | | X | | |
| | 14. Is compliance with the 5S in constant improvement? | | | X | | |
| | 15. Does everyone you ask understand what the 5S consists of? | | | | X | |
| | **TOTAL** | 0 | 10 | 21 | 12 | 0 |

*(1) Deficient. Nothing was done on this concept.*
*(2) Regular. Indications that it is necessary to work with greater effort.*
*(3) Good. There are areas or aspects to improve.*
*(4) Very well. With some sign of not being 100% finished.*
*(5) Excellent. The standards established for the 5'S are met.*

**Result:** **57%**
*(Total amount / 75) x 100*

# Bibliographic references


- *Pillars of the Visual Workplace: The Sourcebook for 5S Implementation.* Hiroyuki Hirano. Productivity Press.
- *5S for Operators: 5 pillars of the visual workplace.* The productivity press development team. Productivity Press.

**Manual de gestión aduanera. Normativas y procedimientos clave del comercio internacional**

*Pedro Coll*

**Cómo participar en ferias comerciales**

*Cristina Peña Andrés*

**Manual del comercio electrónico**

*Eva María Hernández Ramos, Luis Carlos Hernández Barrueco*

**Manual de estrategia de operaciones**

*Ángel Caja Corral*

**Cerebro, inteligencias y mapas mentales**

*Zoraida G. de Montes, Laura Montes G.*

**La Industria 4.0 en la sociedad digital**

*Antoni Garrell Guiu, Llorenç Guilera Agüera*

**Manual de transporte para el comercio internacional**

*Cristina Peña Andrés*

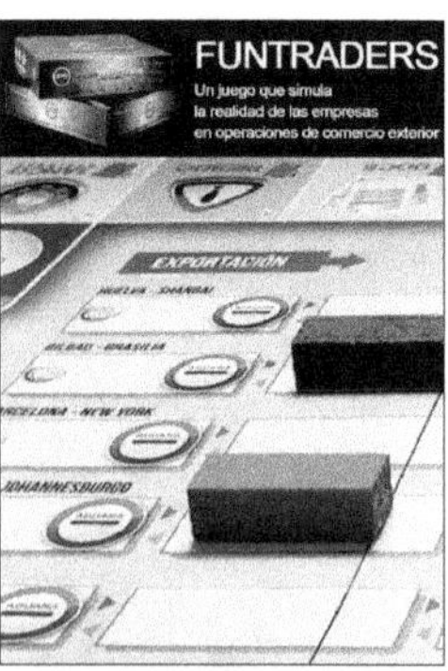

**Manual de gestión de almacenes**

*Sergi Flamarique*

**FUNTRADERS Un juego para aprender comercio internacional**

**Lean Six Sigma. Sistema de gestión para liderar empresas**
*Luis Socconini, Carlo Reato*

**Lean Company. Más allá de la manufactura**
*Luis Socconini*

**Anatomía de la creatividad**
*Llorenç Guilera Agüera*

**Lean Energy 4.0. Guía de Implementación**
*Luis Socconini, Juan Pablo Martín*

**Lean Manufacturing. Paso a paso**
*Luis Socconini*

**Lean Services. Certification Manual**
*Luis Socconini*

**Lean Six Sigma Yellow Belt. Manual de certificación**
*Luis Socconini*

**Lean Six Sigma Green Belt. Manual de certificación**
*Luis Socconini*

**Lean Six Sigma Black Belt. Manual de certificación**
*Luis Socconini*

València, 558 – 08026 Barcelona – Tel. +34-931 429 486 – marge@margebooks.com – www.margebooks.com